THE PANIC OF 1893

THE PANIC OF 1893

In January, 1893, there was a feeling of unease, of uncertainty, everywhere. Low farm prices and crop failures, plus strikes by steelworkers, miners, and railroad men, had depressed business in the United States. A severe business depression in Europe and Australia also cut down the sales of American products abroad. At the same time, European bankers who had loaned millions of dollars to American businessmen now stopped lending them money. This action sent a shock wave through the country. Prices plummeted as people fearfully hoarded the money they had and worried about what tomorrow might bring. Then, one by one, railroads, factories, mills, stores, and banks went broke. The nation — slowly but surely — was about to enter the wildest four years in its peacetime history. By the summer of 1894, 4 million men out of a population of about 65 million were vainly seeking work. The depression was the worst since 1873, and a worse one would not come along until the 1930s.

PRINCIPALS

OLIVER H. KELLEY, who founded the Patrons of Husbandry, known as the Grangers, in 1867.

URIAH S. STEPHENS, who organized the Noble Order of the Knights of Labor in 1869.

GOVERNOR JOHN PETER ALTGELD, whose fight for labor rights and against injustice in Illinois ruined his political career.

SAMUEL GOMPERS, who organized the American Federation of Labor in 1881.

NELSON W. ALDRICH, senator from Rhode Island, who believed that senators should speak for steel, copper, railroads, banks, and other business interests rather than for their states.

MARY E. LEASE, Populist orator, who advised the discontented farmers of the West to "raise less corn and more hell!"

JAMES B. WEAVER, Populist candidate for President, who startled the Republicans and Democrats by polling over a million votes in the 1892 election.

GROVER CLEVELAND, who was the only man to win two nonconsecutive terms as President (1885–89 and 1893–97).

JACOB S. COXEY, a rich quarry owner of Massillon, Ohio, who led an "army" of jobless men to Washington to ask Congress and the President for aid in 1894.

GEORGE B. PULLMAN, who cut wages but refused to lower rents on houses in his company town and fired union spokesmen who protested his action.

EUGENE V. DEBS, president of the A. F. of L.'s American Railway Union, who supported the Pullman strikers.

J. P. MORGAN, who organized a group of Wall Street bankers to help the government sell bonds and protect the Treasury's gold reserve, an action that turned free-silver Democrats in the West against President Cleveland.

MARK HANNA, millionaire industrialist, who retired from business in 1895 and started planning to make William McKinley President of the United States.

WILLIAM McKINLEY, who lost his seat in Congress when voters protested the McKinley Tariff in 1890, then returned to Ohio, was elected governor twice, and made a prolabor record which helped him in the presidential election.

WILLIAM JENNINGS BRYAN, whose stirring "cross of gold" speech helped him win the Democratic presidential nomination over "Silver Dollar Dick" Bland.

Conditions which spawned the Panic of 1893 are typified in this Thomas Nast cartoon of a bird of prey representing "get-rich-quick" businessmen and politicians. The caption read: "How much longer will these birds be allowed to gorge themselves on the savings of the self-denying and industrious — and escape the consequences?"

A FOCUS BOOK

The Panic of 1893

*A time of Strikes, Riots, Hobo Camps,
Coxey's "Army," Starvation, Withering Droughts,
and Fears of "Revolution"*

by Frank B. Latham

Illustrated with contemporary prints

FRANKLIN WATTS, INC.
845 Third Avenue, New York, N.Y. 10022

FOR LUCILLE and LINDA

SBN 531-01022-8
Copyright © 1971 by Franklin Watts, Inc.
Library of Congress Catalog Card Number: 70-132067
Printed in the United States of America
2 3 4 5 6

Contents

THE PANIC OF 1893

Gold reserves were fast dwindling in early 1893. Sketch by T. de Thulstrup in Harper's Weekly *shows inside of a treasury vault in Washington, D. C.*

A Time of Trouble

No frantic newspaper headlines announcing the failure of a great bank or the sudden collapse of stock-market prices signaled the beginning of the Panic of 1893. Twenty years before, the Panic of 1873, which began with the crash of the banking firm of Jay Cooke and Company of Philadelphia and New York, was felt throughout the country within a few days. It knocked over businesses as if they were a row of dominos. The Great Depression of the 1930s, which started with the stock-market crash of October, 1929, brought ruin to owners of stocks all over the land. But the Panic of 1893 was, at first, a silent panic that approached quietly but did its work just as devastatingly.

In January, 1893, there was a feeling of unease and uncertainty everywhere. Businessmen had borrowed heavily to expand their factories and mills and to buy stocks in railroads and other big corporations. They were counting on a rise in prices to help them pay off their debts and make a profit. But low farm prices and crop failures, plus strikes by steelworkers, miners, and railroad men, had upset business in the United States. A severe business depression in Europe and Australia had also cut down the sales of American products abroad. At the same time, European bankers who had loaned millions of dollars to American businessmen stopped lending them money. This action sent a shock wave through the country.

[3]

Prices took another dive as people fearfully hoarded the money they had and worried about what tomorrow might bring. Then, one by one, railroads, factories, mills, and stores went broke. The nation — slowly but surely — was about to enter the wildest four years in its peacetime history.

It was a time of strikes and riots, pitting troops against desperate workers; of bitter threats by farmers as they burned corn for fuel, rather than ship it to market at a loss; of ragged lines of hungry, jobless men straggling through silent factory towns; of angry street-corner speakers who charged that the greedy, get-rich-quick schemes of business had brought the nation to disaster; of tense meetings where businessmen talked fearfully of "a coming revolution."

The first business failures were among the railroads, which had over-built their tracks on borrowed money. The Philadelphia & Reading Railroad went bankrupt in February, 1893. It was followed into bankruptcy by the Erie, the Northern Pacific, the Union Pacific, and the Santa Fe. Within months, 74 railroads operating more than 30,000 miles of track went broke. (Before the depression ended, 156 railroads were to go bankrupt.) Banks with heavy investments in the railroads soon felt the pinch. They started demanding that all borrowers pay off their loans. Businesses that could not pay went into bankruptcy. During the melancholy year of 1893, more than 15,000 companies failed, and 574 banks closed their doors, wiping out the savings of thousands of people. By the summer of 1894, 4 million jobless men out of a population of about 65 million were vainly seeking work. The depression was the worst since 1873, and a worse one would not come along until the 1930s.

The Panic of 1893 and the resulting depression were particularly severe in the agricultural areas of the nation. For example, in the West and in the South, which had far fewer banks than the rest of the country, 153 of these institutions closed their doors.

Farm Problems

The farmers of the West and of the South had been having their ups and downs ever since the Civil War. Prices of crops rose and fell, and good growing weather for a year or two was followed by scorching droughts lasting the next two or three. In fact, since 1865, the farmers had had more downs than ups. Now, in 1893, they were heavily in debt to the banks and to Eastern insurance companies for money they had borrowed. And they depended on the sale of wheat, corn, cotton, hogs, and cattle to get the money to pay their debts.

During the Civil War, Western farmers had been able to sell their crops at high prices and pay their debts easily. But after the war, prices began to fall, slowly but surely. There were price rises in the late 1870s and the early 1880s, but, in general, the trend of prices was down, down, *down*. Wheat that sold for as much as $2 a bushel in 1865 brought only 50 cents twenty-five years later. Corn that sold for 75 cents a bushel in 1869 sold for 28 cents in 1890. Southern farmers found that their cotton, which cost six to seven cents a pound to produce, was selling for five cents a pound in the 1890s. In 1865, a wheat farmer had been able to pay off a $1,000 debt with 500 bushels. But it took around 1,500 bushels to pay off the same debt when wheat prices hit the bottom.

The downward trend in farm prices after 1865 was caused by overproduction. Consider wheat, for example. New wheat-growing regions in the West were opened to cultivation. The use of labor-saving machinery also greatly increased the output of American farms. In addition, India and Australia started growing wheat, and the Russian output, which had been hurt by bad weather, also increased in the 1890s. The supply of wheat exceeded the demand for it, and naturally prices fell.

For the farmer, wheat and other crops were the measure of his labor — long days of work under a hot sun. And he expected the government to provide a supply of currency (money) that would raise prices and give him a fair return for his labor. Whatever the cause of low prices, the farmers believed the government could raise prices by issuing more money. They looked at the money problem as a case of supply and demand. That is, if money was scarce, its value would rise and prices would fall. But if money was plentiful, its value would fall and prices would rise. Thus the farmers favored any and all plans to increase the amount of money issued by the government. A plentiful supply of cheaper money would cause prices to rise and make the farmers' debts easier to pay. But one man's debt is another man's income. So the banker and other lenders of money did not want a farmer paying his debts in less valuable money. They wanted the government to limit the amount of money in circulation. Then this more valuable money would give them a bigger return on the money they loaned. This battle over money was to keep American politics in an uproar for thirty-five years from 1865 to 1900.

At first, the farmers had pinned their hopes for plentiful money on the continued use of greenbacks. During the Civil War, the United States government was unable to pay all the costs of that conflict by taxation and borrowing. In this emergency, the government issued paper money, called "legal tender" notes or greenbacks. This currency was not backed up by either gold or silver in the Treasury. Its value depended on the government's promise to pay the holder of a greenback its full value after

[6]

the war ended. The worth of the greenback also depended on the people's confidence in the government's ability to pay. During the dark days of the war, when the Union armies were bogged down, people's confidence in the government fell and so did the value of the greenback. At times, it was worth less than 50 cents on the dollar, so prices went up. In 1864, it took $12 to buy as much food, clothing, and other necessities as $8 would have bought in 1860. The rise in prices (inflation) aided the farmer. His crops brought high prices, and he could pay his debts with cheap greenbacks.

Aside from issuing greenbacks, the government obtained a great deal of money by selling bonds. To boost bond sales and provide a sounder currency, Congress, in 1863, passed the National Bank Act, which set up a national banking system. Before 1863, the banking business of the nation was in the state-chartered banks. There were 1,600 state banks in 1862, and 1,500 of them were issuing paper money of doubtful value. There were around 7,000 kinds of bank money in circulation and about 4,000 counterfeit varieties were reported.

Under the National Bank Act, a group of men could get a charter for a national bank if they bought government bonds. Whereupon, this new bank could issue paper money (national bank notes) to the value of 90 percent of the bonds the bank's owners bought and deposited with the United States Treasury. The government paid interest to the bank on the bonds it had bought. At the same time, the bank could lend its national bank notes and collect interest from borrowers. This gave the bank a double profit on its money, causing angry farmers to say it was a perfect example of "eating your cake and having it too."

To strengthen the national banks, Congress in 1865 levied a tax of 10 percent on the money issued by state banks. This tax quickly put the state banks out of the business of issuing money. So, except for greenbacks, U.S. paper currency consisted of national bank notes on the na-

[7]

tional debt (government bonds bought by the national banks). Tying our money supply mainly to the national debt brought complaints from farmers in the 1880s. During that time, the government cut down the national debt by paying off the holders of its bonds. This cut down on the amount of bonds held by national banks, thus reducing the amount of national bank notes the banks could issue. As money became scarcer, prices took another drop and farmers felt the pinch. In those days, farmers used paper money, not checks drawn on banks, to pay their bills, and the shortage of currency sorely handicapped them.

The farmers also objected to another provision of the banking act. It required that banks in towns of a population of less than 6,000 had to have a capital of at least $50,000 to do business. The result was that there were few national banks in farming areas. The wiping out of state bank money by the tax of 1865 also drove many small banks in rural areas out of business.

With good reason, the farmers felt that the national banks were not set up to help them. In fact, the failure of the national banks to serve the farmers caused much of their agitation for cheap money.

When the Civil War ended, there was more than 400 million dollars' worth of greenbacks in people's hands. Farmers wanted the government to keep the greenbacks in circulation and also to issue more. But the bankers and other holders of government bonds wanted no greenbacks at all. Calling themselves "sound money" men, they urged the government to return to the gold standard, under which all currency would be backed by gold in the Treasury.

Despite the demands of the farmers, Congress in 1866 passed a law requiring the Treasury to withdraw greenbacks from circulation as fast as they were collected in payment of taxes or other debts owed the government. The angry farmers did not give up their fight for "easy money." During the 1870s, they formed the Greenback party and later joined the

[8]

Greenback Labor party. It demanded the substitution of greenbacks for all other currency, including the money of the hated national banks. Greenback Labor candidates polled thousands of votes and fourteen won seats in the House of Representatives. Congress finally agreed to keep 346 million dollars' worth of greenbacks in circulation at all times. The friends of cheap money celebrated their victory with this song:

> "Thou Greenback, 'tis of thee,
> Fair money of the free,
> Of thee we sing."

However, the fruits of this victory soon turned sour. Seeing that they could not stop the circulation of greenbacks, "sound money" men got Congress to pass the Resumption of Specie Act in 1875. Under this act, the Government promised to redeem in specie (gold coin) all paper money, including greenbacks, which was presented to the Treasury on or after January 1, 1879. Since the greenbacks were redeemable in gold, their value quickly rose, and the frustrated farmers saw another dream of cheap money and high prices disappear.

After 1879, many farmers deserted the Greenback Labor party and flocked to leaders who promised them aid through the free coinage of silver. The Silverites pointed out that, under the Constitution, Congress was given power to coin money while the states were forbidden to make anything but gold and silver legal tender in the payment of debts. Evidently, the Founding Fathers favored bimetallism (the use of both metals). But the difficulty in using a bimetallic system of currency lay in keeping gold and silver on the same level of value so that both would be used by the buyers and sellers of goods. Clearly, if the gold in a gold dollar was worth more on the market than the silver in a silver dollar, people would hoard gold coins and use silver in buying goods and paying

[9]

debts. This behavior of gold and silver was explained by Sir Thomas Gresham, an English financier. "Gresham's law" states that if several kinds of money are in use, the cheaper money will drive the more valuable into hiding. And no amount of oratory or laws proposed by the Silverites could make gold and silver behave the way they wanted them to. For example, Congress in 1792 had fixed the ratio of the two metals at 1 to 15 — one ounce of gold was worth 15 ounces of silver. But it soon became clear that gold had been undervalued, so it was hoarded and the less valuable silver was brought to the mint for coinage. Then, in 1834, the ratio of the two metals was fixed at 16 to 1, and silver was undervalued. Since the silver dollar was worth more than the gold one, banks began paying out gold coins. Silver was not brought to the mint, and many silver dollars were melted down for jewelry and silver plate.

For twenty years preceding 1873, silver was not used as money. Then, in 1873, Congress passed a law stopping the coinage of silver dollars. Silverites later denounced this measure as "the crime of '73." They said it had been secretly passed by Congress to make bankers rich at the expense of farmers. This act had been, however, debated at some length, and one speaker declared: "This bill provides . . . for substituting as legal tender, coin of only one metal instead of two as heretofore."

Outcries against "the crime of '73" came after the production of silver suddenly boomed in several Western states. As silver poured into the market, this metal soon became worth less than gold, and it became profitable to have silver dollars minted. Now, there were attacks on the law ending silver coinage. Owners of silver mines demanded that the government buy silver. They were joined by farmers who saw in this metal an opportunity to increase the supply of money and bring a rise in farm prices.

The fight over silver pitted the bankers and businessmen of the East against the mine owners and the farmers of the West and the South. It also caused trouble in the two major parties; both Democrats and Republicans favored silver. Republican Senator James G. Blaine of Maine insisted that the Constitution required Congress to make gold and silver the money of the land. Representative Richard ("Silver Dollar Dick") Bland, a Democrat of Missouri, rallied support for silver in the West and the South. In 1878, Congress passed a silver measure, the Bland-Allison Act. Republican President Rutherford B. Hayes vetoed the act, but Congress passed it over his veto.

This act required the Treasury to buy between two and four million dollars' worth of silver a month. It further declared that 16 ounces of silver were worth one ounce of gold. But since more silver was being mined than the Treasury was buying, the price of that metal continued to fall. Silver dollars actually were worth about 85 cents in terms of gold. They were, however, legal tender, so people used them to pay taxes and other debts to the government. But holders of government bonds demanded payment in gold. As the Treasury continued to take in silver and pay out gold, its gold reserve began to dwindle. This worry over gold became acute after the election of Democratic President Grover Cleveland in 1884. He was immediately bombarded by arguments from both friends and foes of silver.

"Sound money" men, called "goldbugs" by their foes, urged Cleveland to write a letter saying he opposed the coinage of silver and favored the repeal of the Bland-Allison Act. Cheap money Democrats warned him that an attack on silver would split the party and cause its defeat in the next election. Cleveland ignored this warning and wrote an antisilver letter. It cheered the bankers who were said to be spending sleepless nights counting silver dollars jumping into the Treasury and gold dollars jumping out. Infuriated Silverites said the attack on silver was a bankers' plot to enrich the holders of bonds while squeezing more money out of debt-burdened farmers.

[11]

Before Cleveland took office in March, 1885, the House soundly beat a bill to end the coinage of silver. The vote on this measure was a sure sign of trouble to come for both major parties. Silver was backed by 118 Democrats and 52 Republicans. "Sound money" was supported by 54 Democrats and 64 Republicans. Note that even the Republicans, long defenders of gold, were closely divided over the silver issue. The first battle had been fought in a silver war that was to rage throughout the nation for over ten years.

Despite the successful defense of silver, the problems of mine owners and farmers were not solved. Continued overproduction of silver caused its price to fall again. And overproduction of farm products caused their prices to decline. Finally, the determined Silverites demanded that Congress approve the unlimited coinage of silver at a rate of 16 to 1.

Republican leaders, mainly from the East, blocked the drive for unlimited coinage of silver by getting Congress to pass a compromise measure — the Sherman Silver Purchase Act of 1890. It authorized the Treasury to buy 4½ million ounces of silver a month and pay for them in paper money (silver certificates). This currency could be redeemed at the Treasury in gold or silver. But since the production of silver continued to increase, the Sherman Act did not halt a further fall in silver prices. This act was part of a deal by which the East supported silver in return for the West's support of the McKinley Tariff. This tariff act quickly caused much trouble for the Republicans.

Grangers on the Warpath

While American farmers fought for cheap money, a new farm organization waged a bitter fight against the railroads in the West. The Patrons of Husbandry had been founded in 1867 by Oliver H. Kelley, a government clerk in Washington. Each local unit of this organization was called a Grange, and its members were known as Grangers. Kelley looked upon the Grange merely as a place where the farmers, scattered, as many were, on lonely farms, could get together for a social evening. Soon, however, the Grangers were talking over their problems and seeking ways to solve them. One of their complaints involved the high rates charged by railroads to carry crops to market. Thousands of towns in the West and Midwest were served by only one railroad, which charged what it pleased for its services. Freight charges often took the value of one bushel of wheat to pay the freight on another bushel. The Chicago *Tribune* said: "A few cents change in grain rates made all the difference to the farmers between a good and a losing year."

One Nebraska Granger commented that his state was supposedly owned by the settlers, most of them Civil War veterans. Actually, the state was owned, he said, by insurance companies who held mortgages on the farmers' land, and by the railroads. For they controlled the governor, the legislature, and the courts. One method of control used by the rail-

Complaints of unfair practices by the railroads led Congress to pass an act in 1887 creating the Interstate Commerce Commission. Cartoonist W. A. Rogers, in Harper's Weekly, *depicts the ICC commissioners moving in gingerly to control "Uncle Sam's Wild West (East and South) Show." The railroads successfully resisted most ICC efforts to control their rates and business practices.*

roads was the handing out of free passes to editors, public officials, and their families and friends. Even judges, who had to try railroad cases, and members of state legislatures, who were asked by farmers to regulate the railroads, rode on free passes.

Determined to protect themselves, the Grangers entered politics and elected a large number of representatives to state legislatures. Then they got the legislatures to pass laws regulating railroad rates and banning unfair practices. These so-called Granger laws were quickly challenged in the courts by the railroads.

In 1876, in the case of *Munn v. Illinois*, the United States Supreme Court upheld an Illinois law fixing the maximum prices for the storage of grain in warehouses. The Court declared that "when private property is devoted to public use it is subject to public regulation." On the same day, the Court approved the laws of Illinois, Wisconsin, Iowa, and Minnesota, which fixed the rates for passengers and freight on all railroads in those states. But the Grangers' success against the railroads was short-lived. In 1886, the Supreme Court ruled, in *Wabash Railroad v. Illinois*, that the states did not have the power to regulate nationwide railroads.

Widespread protests by Grangers and other groups led to the passage by Congress of the Interstate Commerce Act of 1886. This act set up the Interstate Commerce Commission to regulate railroad rates and business practices. But the railroads took to the Supreme Court sixteen cases fighting the ICC decisions and won fifteen of them. At the time the Interstate Commerce Act was passed, Senator Nelson W. Aldrich of Rhode Island, a firm defender of big business, called the act "a sham . . . an empty menace to the great interests, made to answer the clamor of the ignorant and the unreasoning."

Summing up the farmers' long struggle against low prices, excessive freight rates, and high interest charges on borrowed money, a Nebraska editor wrote: "We have three crops — corn, freight rates, and interest. The farmers farm the land, and the businessmen farm the farmers."

Big Business on the March

After the Civil War, the watchword of big business was expansion. Expansion of the railroads throughout the country. Expansion in manufacturing, in oil, in mining, and in lumbering. The railroad, the telegraph, more efficient steam engines, and hundreds of labor-saving machines changed the lives of Americans. Small crossroad towns with one store and a church grew into cities boasting dozens of factories. When the Civil War began, the United States ranked fifth in production among the manufacturing nations of the world. By 1890, the United States was challenging Britain for first place. In 1885, Britain led the world in the production of steel. Fourteen years later, Britain's total output was 695,000 tons *less* than that of the Carnegie Steel Company *alone*.

During the 1880s, the wild rush to expand, to produce more and more, ran into the problem that long had bothered the farmers — overproduction. The National Association of Stove Manufacturers reported in 1888: "It is a chronic case of too many stoves and not enough people to buy them." This overproduction brought ruin to many independent American factories. In 1880 for example, the nation had almost 2,000 woolen mills; by 1890, only 1,300. In 1880, there were 1,900 manufacturers of agricultural implements; in 1890, only 900. Competition among the surviving companies grew fierce. It was particularly cutthroat among the railroads. At one time in the 1880s, five railroads were competing for business between New York and Chicago. Two more railroads were being built, and the passenger fare for the trip from New York to Chicago had been beaten down to one dollar. Businessmen finally began forming trusts (combinations of corporations) to control production and fix prices in an industry so that profits would be assured the survivors. An example of a trust at work was given by Judge Barrett of the Supreme Court of New York: "It can close every refinery at will, close some and open others, limit the purchase of raw material, artificially limit the production of refined sugar, enhance the price to enrich themselves and their associates at the public expense, and depress the price when necessary to crush out and impoverish a foolhardy rival."

Farmers and small businessmen who feared the power of the trusts demanded that Congress act against them. In a message to Congress, written after he had been defeated by Republican Benjamin Harrison in the 1888 presidential election, Grover Cleveland angrily denounced the actions of big business: "We discover the existence of trusts, combinations and monopolies, while the citizen is struggling far in the rear, or is trampled to death beneath an iron heel. Corporations, which should be the servants of the people, are fast becoming the people's masters."

Both major parties promised to control the trusts, and in 1890, Congress passed the Sherman Anti-Trust Act. It declared illegal "every contract combination in the form of trust or otherwise or conspiracy in restraint of trade and commerce among the several states or with foreign nations." The act did not define a "trust" or a "conspiracy," and it said little about how action was to be taken against them. In fact, Republican Senator Orville H. Platt of Connecticut hinted strongly that the act was a lot of nonsense. During Senate debate, he said: "The conduct of the Senate . . . has not been in the line of the honest preparations of a bill to prohibit and punish trusts. . . . The whole effort has been to get some bill

[17]

In the 1870s and 1880s, businessmen formed trusts (combinations of corporations) to control production and fix prices in an industry. W. A. Rogers in Harper's Weekly *sees the trusts as many-headed beasts that menace small businessmen and consumers.*

headed, 'A Bill to Punish Trusts' with which to go to the country."

When the act went into operation, it had little or no effect on trusts. Neither President Harrison nor President Cleveland, despite the latter's earlier complaints about trusts, really tried to enforce the Sherman Act.

While the trusts were let alone to fix prices and rake in high profits, they were also protected from the competition of low-priced foreign goods by the tariff. The first tariff had been passed merely to provide revenue for the government. Later, tariffs were passed to protect the "infant industries" of America from foreign competition. These tariffs levied a duty (tax) on foreign products that raised their retail prices and kept them from underselling American-made products. During the Civil War, the Republican-controlled Congress passed several tariff laws that increased duties on foreign goods. The excuse then was that these higher duties raised money needed to pay for the war. But the tariff of 1864 was not a tariff for revenue. It was an out-and-out protective tariff to shield American industry from foreign competition. Despite some tinkering with rates by Congress to quiet protesting farm and labor groups, the rates remained high during the 1870s and 1880s.

Meanwhile, the farmer had to sell his crops in the world market in competition with foreign growers of wheat, corn, cotton, and other products. The farmer could not afford to hold his crops back and wait for a price rise. He could not combine with other farmers of the world to fix prices and control production, as did the sugar trust, the steelmakers, and the railroads in the United States. In fact, as farm prices fell, the American farmer had to grow more wheat, corn, and cotton in a desperate effort to pay his debts.

Labor Unions Fight for Survival

The growth of the factory system in the United States taught workers the need to organize for the protection of their rights. Skilled handicraft workers found their jobs being taken over by machines. Wages were low, hours of work long, housing was foul, and employers gave little thought to their workers' welfare or rights. During the Civil War, the lag between wages and the rising cost of living spurred the organization of unions. By 1869, the number of members in national labor unions totaled 170,000. By 1872, there were around 300,000 trade unionists belonging to thirty-two national unions. The most powerful of these unions were those of the bricklayers, the typesetters, the shoemakers, the iron molders, the miners, and the locomotive engineers. But these so-called national unions had no strong national leadership to direct their members, scattered in towns and cities all over the country. There was no planning for collective bargaining over wages and hours with employers, and no effort made to build up strike funds and benefits for the ill and the injured. As a result of their weak organizations, the national unions were practically wiped out by antiunion employers during the depression of 1873-1879.

Meanwhile, however, efforts had been made to form a labor confederation to give leadership and direction to the national unions. The first such confederation, the National Labor Union, was organized in 1866. But this organization played down the strike and put its faith mainly in cheap money and producers' cooperatives to make and sell goods needed by the workers. W. H. Sylvis, an early leader of the National Labor Union, also favored the formation of a third party that would be supported by workers as well as farmers. A National Labor Reform party was organized, but it made a poor showing in the 1872 election and soon faded away along with the National Labor Union. But this doomed union did accomplish something. It was a forerunner of the Knights of Labor and the American Federation of Labor, and it proved that a confederation of national unions was not an impossible dream. The leaders of the National Labor Union failed to see the need of collective bargaining and the strike to win labor a place in the nation's life. Instead, they wasted their time on campaigns for cheap money and producers' cooperatives.

The Noble Order of the Knights of Labor, which was organized in Philadelphia in 1869 by Uriah S. Stephens, profited by the errors of the National Labor Union. The Knights started out as a secret society of garment cutters in a tailor shop. It grew rapidly and by 1873 had 80 local assemblies of workingmen. The rise of the Knights came at a time when the national labor unions (miners, iron molders, locomotive engineers, and others) were under heavy attack by antiunion employers. They fought the unions with the blacklist (barring the employment of a union member) and the "ironclad oath" (binding a worker not to join a union). Employers also hired spies and strikebreakers and got the aid of the courts against unions. Judges generally looked upon unions as "conspiracies" against the public.

This all-out attack by employers smashed many national unions. Their membership fell from 500,000 in the early 1870s to less than 50,000 in 1878. The heaviest blow was dealt these unions during the "Great Railroad Strike" of 1877. As the railroads lost business during the depression, they started cutting wages. Another slash in wages in July, 1877, plus the use of the blacklist, triggered a strike that spread from the Atlantic Coast to St. Louis. Violence soon swept dozens of cities. At Cumberland, Maryland, the state militia fired on strikers and killed ten of them. Thousands of jobless men belonging to other unions joined the railroad workers out of sympathy. Rioting mobs ran wild in Baltimore for two days. At the request of the governor of Maryland, President Hayes sent Federal troops into the state — the first use of the army in an industrial dispute. Clashes between militia and strikers in Pittsburgh cost the lives of twenty-six men. Before the strike ended, it had spread over 14 states, and the loss of property was estimated at 10 million dollars. The militia, backed by the army, finally restored order. Thus the strike collapsed, and the men lost their fight against pay cuts. In addition, the railroads blacklisted the strikers and used the courts to punish the unions as conspiracies.

Looking for a refuge in this time of trouble, union men joined the Knights of Labor. Its oath of secrecy was a welcome shelter from employers armed with spies, blacklists, and ironclad oaths. Other policies of the Knights also won the support of workers. It stood for industrial unionism instead of craft unionism. An industrial union takes in all workers in an industry regardless of the skill they have or the work they do. But a craft union contains members of one particular trade or craft, such as shoemakers, typesetters, or iron molders. Among the Knights' members were white men and women, black men and women, skilled and unskilled workers, house servants and farmhands.

The Knights opposed the formation of a labor party, but it favored many of the reforms advocated earlier by the National Labor Union. These included an eight-hour workday, producers' cooperatives, abolition of child labor, and a law prohibiting the use by industry of contract laborers from Europe. Labor long had accused employers of trying to beat down the wages of American workers by bringing in labor from

[22]

abroad. Favoring strikes only as a last resort, the Knights believed in arbitration of disputes with employers.

The Knights began a great expansion in membership following the election of Terrence V. Powderly as its Grand Master Workman and the abandonment of secrecy in 1879. Although the Knights of Labor opposed strikes, it soon got involved in several. In 1885, it called a strike that blocked a wage reduction on financier Jay Gould's Wabash railway system. A second strike on the Wabash ended with Gould promising not to use union membership as an excuse for firing workers. This recognition of the Knights by one of the nation's biggest employers of labor brought another sharp rise in the Knights' membership.

The year 1886 marked the high point of the Knights of Labor. It also marked the year of its sudden collapse. During 1886, the nation was swept by strikes involving more than 600,000 men. Alarmed businessmen talked of a "labor uprising," of "revolution." General William T. Sherman, then commander in chief of the Army, predicted: "There will soon come an armed contest between capital and labor. They will oppose each other not with words and arguments and ballots, but with shot and shell and gunpowder and cannon. The better classes are tired of the insane howling of the lower strata, and they mean to stop them." In an editorial, the Chicago *Times* grimly declared that "hand grenades should be thrown among those who are striving to obtain higher wages."

On May 3, 1886, a clash between strikers and strikebreakers at the McCormick Harvester Company in Chicago touched off a riot in which the police killed four labor demonstrators. The next day, a protest meeting was held at Haymarket Square. Several of the speakers were anarchists, who believed that all government is evil and should be opposed by force if necessary. The meeting, described by Mayor Carter Harrison as peaceful, was breaking up when 200 policemen charged into the square. A bomb was thrown and the police fired into the crowd. Eight policemen

[23]

and four protesters were killed. Melville Stone, editor of the Chicago *Daily News*, promptly hired Pinkerton detectives to round up men who were known to be anarchists, and they were put on trial for murder. The throwers of the bomb were never identified, but Judge Joseph E. Gary ruled that anarchists who believed in violence were equally guilty with those who threw the bomb. The jury found eight anarchists guilty, ordering the death penalty for seven and imprisonment for the eighth. Four anarchists were hanged, one committed suicide, and two others had their sentences reduced to life imprisonment. In 1893, the Democratic governor of Illinois, John Peter Altgeld, pardoned the three men who were still alive. Not content with pardoning the men — an act even conservatives were willing to approve if he did it quietly — the courageous Altgeld took the judge and jury to task. He charged that Judge Gary "conducted the trial with malicious ferocity" and allowed some men to serve on the jury even after they admitted that they had already decided that the anarchists were guilty. Altgeld's attack on justice brought savage criticism from newspapers and politicians and ruined his political career.

The Knights of Labor had nothing to do with the Haymarket Riot. But the organization was blamed because it had called strikes that led to violence in Chicago. Public opinion turned against the Knights, many of its members quit, and quarrels among its leaders hastened the collapse of the organization.

One reason for the sudden collapse of the Knights was the existence of another labor organization to which its dissatisfied members could turn. This was the American Federation of Labor, which had been organized in 1881 by a London-born cigar maker named Samuel Gompers. Unlike the Knights, the Federation did not try to organize everyone in big industrial unions. It was a federation of craft unions of skilled workers. The Federation was ready to strike if necessary, but it always sought to persuade employers that face-to-face bargaining over wages and hours was much more sensible. The Federation opposed the formation of a third party and took a hand in politics only to "reward its friends and punish its enemies" on election day. After the collapse of the Knights of Labor, the Federation grew rapidly in membership. In 1889, the Federation's powerful Amalgamated Association of Iron and Steel Workers signed a three-year contract with the Carnegie Steel Company. This was a great victory for the Federation, but during the bitter years of the early 1890s it was to be tested sternly by brutal strikes.

Big Business Finds a Hero

During the 1880s, the hero of the get-rich-quick businessmen was Herbert Spencer, the English philosopher. He provided them with an excuse to go on doing what they were doing. Quoting a phrase from Thomas Paine, "That government is best which governs least," Spencer said that business should be let alone. Government's only job was to provide police and an army and navy. There should be no public education, no limitation of the hours of labor, no welfare legislation. The poor, according to Spencer, were unfit and should be eliminated. "The whole effort of nature is to get rid of such, to clear the world of them, and make room for better." Nature, added Spencer, puts everyone alike on trial: "If they are sufficiently complete to live, they *do* live, and it is well they should live. If they are not sufficiently complete to live, they die, and it is best they should die." In Spencer's grim view of things, the rule of life was the "survival of the fittest."

Spencer's words exactly suited the businessman who had come out on top in the cutthroat competition of the day. That shrewd steelmaker and ferocious competitor, Andrew Carnegie, joyfully accepted Spencer's ideas and went on to shrug off critics of competition. "It is here," Carnegie wrote, "we cannot evade it; no substitute for it has been found; and while the law [of competition] may sometimes be hard for the individual,

[26]

it is best for the race, because it insures the survival of the fittest in every department." Later, Carnegie, who had become the world's richest man, had some second thoughts. "Few millionaires," he wrote, "are clear of the sin of having made beggars."

Spencer's ideas undoubtedly influenced judges when they were called upon to pass on the legality of labor legislation. In 1885, for example, the New York Court of Appeals ruled illegal a law that forbade the making of cigars in tenements. Samuel Gompers of the A. F. of L. had persuaded young Theodore Roosevelt, a member of the New York assembly, to sponsor this act in 1881, and it was signed by Governor Grover Cleveland. It sought to break up the rapidly growing sweatshops in crowded cities, which underpaid and overworked people. The Court of Appeals said it could not understand how "the cigar maker is to be improved in his health or his morals by forcing him from his home and its hallowed and beneficent influences to ply his trade elsewhere." During his investigation of the sweatshop tenements where cigar makers worked, Roosevelt wrote:

"The tobacco was stored everywhere, alongside the foul bedding, and in a corner where there were scraps of food. The men, women, and children in this room worked by day and far into the evening and they slept and ate there. . . ."

The Court of Appeals' comment on the "beneficent influences" of these foul hovels startled Roosevelt. He said he began for the first time to see that the courts were not the best judges of what should be done to improve working conditions.

During this same period, the courts of Pennsylvania, West Virginia, Illinois, Missouri, and Kansas declared illegal laws that forbade mineowners and other employers from paying their men in scrip instead of money. The scrip, except by special arrangement with merchants, could be spent only in company stores, where the employer could charge what suited

Joseph Keppler's cartoon in Puck, *titled "The Bosses of the Senate," contends that the trusts give orders to the lawmakers and run things to suit themselves. In the 1880s and 1890s, there were so many wealthy businessmen in the Senate that it was called the Millionaires' Club.*

him. The unions fought this system, but when they got laws passed against it, the courts said they interfered with the workers' "rights." The Pennsylvania court said, for example, that the law was "an insulting attempt" to put the worker under the protection of the state, "which was not only degrading to his manhood, but invaded his rights as a citizen of the United States."

While businessmen went on doing what came naturally, and the courts backed them up, politicians played follow-the-leader. Big corporations supplied members of Congress with campaign funds, gifts, and bribes. The members in return saw to it that big business got high tariffs, land grants in the West, sound money policies, and freedom from laws regulating the trusts or protecting the rights of labor. Republican Senator Nelson W. Aldrich firmly believed that senators should speak for steel, copper, coal, the railroads, banks, and other business interests rather than for their states. At this time, senators were not elected directly by the people but by the state legislatures. Many of these legislatures were firmly controlled by political bosses who, in turn, took orders from big-business leaders. The legislatures naturally elected senators who were friendly to big business. Instead of getting a man elected who would take orders, many business leaders got themselves elected to the Senate. In the 1880s and 1890s, the Senate was so filled with wealthy businessmen that it was called the "Millionaires' Club." Senator George Hearst looked over these men and confidently declared: "I have traveled a good deal and observed men and things and I have made up my mind after all my experiences that the members of the Senate are the survivors of the fittest."

Farmers and workers were not ready to accept Senator Hearst's kind words. "The United States Senate," declared the Greenbackers, "is a body composed largely of aristocratic millionaires who . . . generally purchased their elections in order to protect the great monopolies which they represent." The Labor party of 1888 took a shot at both major parties: "We denounce the Democratic and Republican parties as hopelessly and shamelessly corrupt and, by reason of their affiliation with monopolies, equally unworthy of the [support] of those who do not live upon public plunder." While Edward Everett Hale was chaplain of the Senate, he was asked, "Do you pray for the Senators?" "No," he said. "I look at the Senators and pray for the country."

The Rise of the Populists

During his first term as President (1885-1889), Cleveland clashed with Congress over the tariff, the pension laws, and the money surplus. In the 1880s, the government regularly collected more money than it spent. This surplus amounted to around 100 million dollars a year. Idle money lay in the Treasury while farmers demanded that more money be put in circulation. The surplus resulted from the failure of Congress to repeal taxes imposed during the Civil War and from the high duties levied by the protective tariff. Gradually, Congress repealed the war taxes, but the tariff continued to pour money into the Treasury. The Republican Congress then hit upon a shrewd way to get rid of this embarrassing surplus. It gave generous pensions to Civil War veterans, with the result that the grateful veterans voted for Republican candidates on election day.

The first pension law gave a pension to any veteran who claimed to have been disabled during the war. Year after year, Congress revised the law to increase benefits and make more veterans eligible. In the 1880s, the veterans' organization, the Grand Army of the Republic, demanded pensions based on service, not disability. Cleveland vetoed such a pension bill in 1887, and the House failed to override his veto. The President bluntly said that the way to get rid of the surplus was to cut tariff duties, not to give the surplus to veterans. But the Republicans solidly opposed any cut in duties and were joined by Democrats who wanted to protect industries in their states.

Cleveland's defeat in 1888 by Republican Benjamin Harrison, a war veteran, was due as much to the hostility of the veterans as to the opposition of businessmen who wanted to keep tariff duties high.

The confident Republicans looked upon their victory over Cleveland as the triumph of the protection principle in writing tariffs. So a handsome young Representative named William McKinley of Ohio immediately went to work on a new tariff that would please those industries that had backed the Republicans in 1888. As already noted, Eastern Republicans backed the Sherman Silver Purchase Act in return for Western support of the McKinley Tariff Act of 1890. When Congress got through with the McKinley Tariff, it was protection run wild. On many products, the new duties were so high that imports were excluded altogether. The McKinley Tariff even protected one industry that did not exist. There was no tin-plate industry in the nation, but duties were levied on tin plate. Early U.S. protective tariffs sought to aid "infant industries." The 1890 tariff protected one industry that had not even been born!

To quiet the farmers, the tariff duties on wheat, corn, potatoes, and eggs were raised. But this was just so much window dressing to hide the fact that nothing was done for the farmer. Foreign producers were not shipping wheat, corn, potatoes, and eggs to the United States. Furthermore, overproduction of wheat and corn had driven the prices of those crops down, and no tariff duty would help raise them. The duty on wool was also increased, but wool growing was limited mostly to Ohio.

The duty on steel rails raised the price of English rails by $28. So an American steel company could increase its price by $27 and still undersell its English competitor. The duty on rails helped steelmakers pile up millions of dollars in profits, but their workers' lot did not improve. The work remained hard, brutal, and dangerous. Great care was lavished

[31]

To reduce an embarrassing surplus piled up in the Treasury by the high tariff, and to win votes on election day, the Republican-controlled Congress voted generous pensions to Civil War veterans. C. J. Taylor in Puck *shows James Tanner, the most generous of the pension commissioners, operating his "Horn of Plenty."*

on the buildings and machinery of the steel plants while the workers were forced to live in pigsties.

Not without reason did farmers and workers call the McKinley measure a "rich man's tariff." Republicans insisted that the tariff would aid the worker through higher wages, but prices immediately went up faster than wages. Even a leading Republican, Senator Shelby Cullom of Illinois, grumbled that hundreds of American-made products that were protected by high duties "are sold in foreign markets at from 25 to 60 percent less than is charged to the American consumer." During the 1890 campaign to elect members to Congress, the Democrats attacked the McKinley Tariff by peddling 25-cent tin dippers for one dollar. When a duty had been placed on tin plate, immediate steps were taken to create an American tin-plate industry. This brought new business to the manufacturers who made the iron sheets that were coated with tin to produce tin plate. But the prices of tinware and tin roofing quickly went up, and Democrats brought this fact home to consumers with their one-dollar tin dippers.

The Republicans were soundly beaten in the 1890 election. Their majority in the Senate was cut to eight votes, while the Democrats took control of the House, winning 235 seats to the Republicans' 88. William McKinley was among those Republicans who were defeated. Easterners who had paid little attention to the farmers' angry complaints over scarce money and low prices were startled by the election. *Harper's Weekly* called the results "stunning." Among the newcomers in the House was thirty-year-old William Jennings Bryan of Nebraska, a brilliant orator with an electrifying voice. Bryan had won by a landslide in a district that was safely Republican two years earlier.

More disturbing to the Republicans than the Democrats' gains was the victory of nine representatives and two senators who carried the banner of the People's (or Populist) party. The main strength of this party

[33]

was in Kansas, Nebraska, and the Dakotas, but it had also swept over into Minnesota and Iowa.

This third-party movement was the outgrowth of the National Farmers' Alliance (known as the Northwestern Alliance). It won the support of Grangers, members of the Knights of Labor, supporters of free silver, Greenbackers, and other reform groups. Meanwhile, in the South and Southwest, several farm organizations combined to form the National Farmers' Alliance and Industrial Union (known as the Southern Alliance).

In 1890, members of the Northwestern Alliance went into politics with a bang. In Kansas, the farmers carried the banner of the People's party. They called themselves the People's Independent party in Nebraska, and the Independent party in South Dakota.

A fiery group of leaders rallied the farmers to the People's party in Kansas. There was "Sockless Jerry" Simpson, editor W. A. Peffer, the champion whisker grower of the West, and Mary E. Lease who declared: "What you farmers need to do is raise less corn and more hell!" And the farmers did raise hell on election day. They elected five Populist congressmen and sent W. A. Peffer to Washington to replace Senator J. J. Ingalls. The Populists also took control of the lower house of the Kansas legislature. Throughout the South and West, candidates supported by the Farmers' Alliances were sent to Congress and state legislatures. Alliance members elected "Pitchfork Ben" Tillman governor of South Carolina and sent a senator and a majority of the state's representatives to Congress. In several Southern states, at least twenty-five victorious Democratic congressmen promised to support Alliance policies. In South Dakota, the Independent party elected the Reverend J. M. Kyle to the United States Senate. In the West, a total of eight candidates calling themselves Populists or Independents were elected to Congress.

At St. Louis, on February 22, 1892, representatives of the two National Farmers' Alliances, as well as delegates from labor groups, organized the national People's party, also called the Populists. Although it lasted but a few years, it was the most influential third party in American history. (The Republican party was a third party when it was founded in 1854, but it quickly became a major party after the 1856 election.) Ignatius Donnelly of Minnesota wrote the Populist call for action that brought shouts of approval from the West and South. "We meet in the midst of a nation brought to the verge of moral, political and material ruin," wrote Donnelly. "Corruption dominates the ballot box, the legislatures, the Congress, and touches even [the courts]. . . . The fruits of the toil of millions are boldly stolen to build up colossal fortunes for a few. . . . Governmental injustice [breeds] the two great classes of tramps and millionaires. . . ."

Then, on July 4, in Omaha, Nebraska, the People's party issued its "Declaration of Independence" from the major parties. The declaration consisted of the Populists' platform of promises to the voters. It demanded: the free and unlimited coinage of silver and gold at the present legal ratio of 16 to 1; a flexible currency controlled by the government and not by the privately owned national banks; a graduated income tax (based on ability to pay); a government parcel-post system to break the hold of the great express companies; restriction of immigration in order to raise the wages of labor; the direct election of United States senators by the people (to curb the power of political bosses); the secret Australian ballot (to keep political bosses and employers from making sure that workers voted "right"); the initiative, whereby legislation may be proposed by a vote of the people, and the referendum, whereby bills passed by the legislature may be approved or rejected by the voters in a special election; government ownership of the railroads, the telephone, and the telegraph; produce subtreasuries where farmers could put their crops when prices were low and receive paper money from the Treasury; the

[35]

return to the government of all land owned by noncitizens or "by railroads and other corporations in excess of their actual needs." A look at past history will show why the Populist demand for the reform of the government's land policy set the nerves of big business on edge. Congress had set out in 1862 to aid the landless and wound up helping the rich get richer.

The Homestead Act, passed by Congress in 1862, gave to heads of families or individuals twenty-one years of age or over a quarter section (160 acres) of land after a five-year period of residence and cultivation. No charge per acre was required unless the homesteader wanted to speed up the grant of title to his land. If he wanted to do this, he could buy his farm outright after six months' residence at a price of $1.25 an acre. Eighty acres were all the land a farmer needed to make a living on the well-watered lands of the Midwest. But he needed much more than 160 acres to get by on the dry, windswept high plains of Kansas and other Western states. Thousands of homesteaders gave up the fight and were bought out by cattlemen. Cattle companies frequently took over thousands of acres of public land while government agents looked the other way.

In an effort to help the homesteader, the Timber Culture Act of 1873 granted him an additional 160 acres if he planted a quarter of it in trees within ten years. Then, in 1877, the cattle companies persuaded Congress to pass the Desert Land Act. For a total of $1.25 an acre, and a promise to irrigate the land within three years, a person could obtain 640 acres within certain Western states. Much of this was good grazing land, and the cattle companies grabbed most of it. In 1891, the act was extended to Colorado, very little of which state could be claimed to be "desert land." The final raid on public lands in the 1870s came with the passage of the Timber and Stone Act of 1878. A quarter section of land "unfit for cultivation" could be bought by any person for $2.50 an acre. This act benefited the big lumber companies, not the homesteaders.

To encourage the building of railroads in the West, Congress voted a total of 158 million acres of land to these companies. Instead of making this land available to settlers on fair terms, many railroads held out choice sections waiting for a rise in prices. The Southern Pacific tried to sell land to settlers at $25 to $40 an acre instead of $2.50, the government price. The Santa Fe, on the other hand, sold German Mennonites in Kansas 60,000 acres at about $4 an acre. It also built the Mennonites temporary shelters and gave them several sections of land so that they could set up a "poor" fund.

In 1890, all land grants not used by the railroads had been declared forfeited to the government. But the railroads went to court to fight the government and not more than two million acres were ever returned.

The Populists' platform brought cries of horror from big business. But except for free silver and government ownership of the railroads, telephone, and telegraph, all of its other proposals were approved in whole or in part by Congress and state legislatures within the next thirty years.

The Populists were not revolutionists, but they did want a house-cleaning that would make the system of private ownership and operation of property work better for farmers and labor. Senator W. A. Peffer of Kansas bluntly declared: "The farmer has been the victim of a gigantic scheme of spoilation. Never before was such a vast aggregation of brains and money brought to bear to force men into labor for the benefit of the few." And dozens of Populist speakers told huge crowds in the West and South that "the railroad corporations will either own the people or the people will own the railroads."

"Crazy" was the mildest adjective most newspapers used to describe the Populists. Theodore Roosevelt called Senator Peffer "a well-meaning, pinheaded, anarchistic crank." Alarmed businessmen stopped the million-aire industrialist Marcus Alonso Hanna on the street in Cleveland and asked if they should sell their railroad stocks immediately. Hanna smiled and said: "You make me think of a lot of scared hens." A wealthy woman in New York City told the famous humorist John Kendrick Bangs that all Populists should be tried for treason and jailed. When Bangs wanted to know just what they had done, the woman could only sputter and say: "Everything!"

While the Populist platform sent nervous conservatives into temper tantrums, its presidential candidate in 1892 aroused little concern. He was General James B. Weaver of Iowa, a dignified longtime campaigner for cheap money and the Greenback candidate for the Presidency in 1880. His running mate as Vice-President was General James G. Field, a Confederate soldier.

Cleveland Wins — Labor Loses

In June, 1892, the Republicans met in convention at Minneapolis and renominated President Harrison. Many Republican party bosses did not like the mild-mannered, well-meaning Harrison. But he had taken orders for four year and kept quiet most of the time. So the party could not dump him without making itself look bad. A few leaders hinted to William McKinley that he could have the nomination, but he decided that this was not the time to run for President. His adviser was Mark Hanna of Cleveland, Ohio. The Hanna-McKinley team would be heard from again in a few years. The Republican platform praised the McKinley Tariff and the Sherman Anti-Trust Act. The ticklish money question was handled in a way to avoid trouble. The party called for the use of "both gold and silver" and said every dollar, "paper or coin," should be equally good.

The Democrats met in Chicago later in June and nominated Grover Cleveland to run for President a third time. Adlai E. Stevenson of Illinois was nominated for Vice-President. (His grandson ran for President in 1952 and 1956, losing to Dwight D. Eisenhower.)

Opposition to the McKinley Tariff helped win Cleveland the nomination, but he was not happy about the party platform blast at the tariff. Sounding like the Populists, the Democrats declared: "We denounce

[39]

Republican protection as a fraud, a robbery of the great majority of the American people for the benefit of the few. . . ." Cleveland feared that such an outspoken statement would cost him votes in industrial states and lead to his defeat.

The platform promise on money got back to the old-style language that could be read two ways. It spoke of "both metals" in a way that seemed to promise free silver to the West and a dollar "good as gold" to the East. Eastern bankers and businessmen were satisfied because they knew Cleveland had long opposed free silver. Democrats took Cleveland as the only man who could beat the Republicans. The party sought to soothe the West by nominating Stevenson, who favored silver.

The 1892 election was expected to be close, but Cleveland scored an easy victory. The big surprise, however, was the excellent showing made by the Populists in their first national election. Weaver polled over a million votes and won the electoral votes of Colorado, Idaho, Kansas, and Nevada. In the Western states, where they were weak, the Democrats threw their support to the Populists. But in the South, the conservative Democrats, called Bourbons, bitterly fought the People's party. A speaking tour by Weaver and Mary E. Lease was marked by catcalls and flying rocks and eggs. Mrs. Lease later remarked that Georgians made Weaver look like "a regular walking omelet." Weaver was unpopular because, as a Union officer, he had served in the South after the Civil War. Mrs. Lease was opposed by those who disliked female politicians. A huge woman, nearly six feet tall, with a compelling voice, Mrs. Lease did not discourage easily. William Allen White, the rising young editor of the Emporia (Kansas) *Gazette*, glumly observed that she could "recite the multiplication table and set a crowd to hooting or hurrahing at her will."

In Georgia and Alabama, the Bourbon Democrats won by herding Negroes to the polls and seeing that they voted the Democratic ticket.

[40]

Later, Tom Watson of Georgia, "Pitchfork Ben" Tillman of South Carolina, and other Populist leaders punished the Negroes by getting state constitutions amended to deny them the vote.

Although the Populists hurt the Republicans in the West, they actually lost the election in the big Eastern states. Here, workers compared their low wages to the high prices in the stores and blamed the McKinley Tariff. The Democrats kept their anger hot by peddling their 25-cent tin dippers for one dollar. In the 1870s and 1880s, low farm prices had aided labor by keeping food costs down. But by the 1890s, "real wages" — measured not only by dollars but by the cost of rent, food, clothing, and other goods — had begun to decline. So labor started paying more attention to the farmer's complaints about the tariff and the trusts.

The labor policies of the Republican vice-presidential candidate, Whitelaw Reid, also proved harmful to the party. A strike at Reid's newspaper, the New York *Tribune*, dragged on during the election campaign and cost the Republicans votes in New York. Even more damaging was the bloody strike at the Homestead plant of the Carnegie Steel Company.

As already noted, the A.F. of L.'s Amalgamated Association of Iron and Steel Workers had signed a history-making three-year contract with Carnegie in 1889. The Amalgamated, with 24,000 skilled workers as members, was probably the most powerful union of its day. When the time came to write a new contract for the Homestead plant, the company balked at granting pay raises. Andrew Carnegie and Henry C. Frick, the 41-year-old chairman of the company, argued that the use of labor-saving machines warranted a cut in wages. That was the announced reason for the quarrel that led to the strike. But there is evidence that Carnegie and Frick resented the union's power and were ready to challenge it. In 1886, Carnegie had written magazine articles that were mildly prolabor. Now,

[41]

however, he backed Frick against the union. Hoping to split the unskilled, nonunion workers away from the skilled union men, Frick announced that he would close the plant on July 1 and reopen it on July 6 with nonunion workers. He then prepared for trouble by surrounding the plant with a high fence topped with barbed wire. He also arranged secretly for 300 armed Pinkerton guards to be brought up the Monongahela River from Pittsburgh on two barges.

The unskilled majority of the workers surprised Frick by siding with the union men. They seized the plant and also took control of the town. When the Pinkerton barges appeared, the strikers opened fire and the battle lasted all day. Three Pinkertons and ten strikers were wounded. Finally, the Pinkertons surrendered and were allowed to leave Homestead by train. On July 12, the Pennsylvania National Guard took over Homestead. Strikebreakers were hired, and Frick reopened the plant on July 15. The wounding of Frick by Alexander Berkman, an anarchist who was not a striker, turned public opinion against the union. On November 20, the union called off the strike. Only about a fifth of the original Carnegie employees were rehired. Other steel companies then refused to recognize the union and thus it was smashed.

When Frick was wounded, Carnegie, who was in Scotland, cabled that he was coming home. Frick urged him to stay in Scotland and then told the newspapers that he would "never recognize the union, never, never." Carnegie realized that if he came home, Frick would resign. So he remained in Scotland and publicly supported Frick. Privately, in a letter to Prime Minister William E. Gladstone of Britain, Carnegie wrote that the hiring of strikebreakers "was a foolish step. . . . The pain I suffer increases daily. The works [plant] are not worth one drop of human blood. . . ."

During the strike, Carnegie's prolabor statements were denounced as fakery. The St. Louis *Post-Dispatch* said: "In the estimation of nine-

[42]

tenths of the thinking people . . . he has confessed himself a moral coward."

Carnegie may have liked his men and sympathized with them. There is evidence that many of his workers respected and loved him even after the strike ended. But he permitted Frick, the hardheaded man who put machines ahead of workers, to set policy at Homestead. Frick was another of those ambitious men who believed in the "survival of the fittest."

A puzzling man was Andrew Carnegie. He could ruin a business rival or smash a union, and then give nearly all of his immense fortune away for, as he wrote, "the good of my fellow men."

A Party Divided, a Nation in Trouble

The victorious Democrats in 1892 chanted: "Grover! Grover! Four more years of Grover! Out they go, in we go; then we'll be in clover!" Unfortunately, there proved to be more poison ivy than clover in the Democrats' future. When Cleveland took office on March 4, 1893, the Democratic party had a majority in both houses of Congress for the first time since the Civil War. As a result, impatient farmers and workers in factories and mills expected the Democrats to keep the promises they had made during the campaign. The big trouble was that the Democrats could not agree on just what they had promised to do for the voters. Cleveland was known to oppose high tariffs, free silver, and bigger pensions. But many Democratic senators from industrial states liked the McKinley Tariff. Western senators favored free silver to aid the farmers. And few Democrats wanted to arouse the short-tempered veterans by slashing pension payments.

Cleveland's plan of sitting tight and opposing things was not enough at a time when the country was boiling with discontent. Wages were too low for the working man to support his family decently. Farm prices had taken another tumble while the farmers' debts grew more burdensome each year. Low wages and low farm incomes cut the purchasing power

[44]

of millions of consumers, and goods began to pile up on store shelves. Fewer customers meant trouble for businessmen, who had borrowed money to buy more machines and increase production. During the rapid expansion of American factories, mills, mines, and railroads after the Civil War, businessmen had borrowed huge sums of money by selling bonds to European bankers. Cloudy days for American business appeared in 1890 when the Argentine government failed to pay interest on millions of dollars' worth of bonds it had sold to English bankers. The great English banking firm of Baring Brothers failed, and during the resulting "Baring panic," hard-pressed bankers sold American bonds to get ready cash. The sale of these bonds, which were payable in gold, drained that valuable metal from the United States Treasury. Worried by signs of trouble in American farming and the widespread strikes in industry in 1892, foreign bankers sold more of their American bonds. The drain of gold from the Treasury increased alarmingly.

The operation of the Sherman Silver Purchase Act also put heavy pressure on the gold reserves of the Treasury. Despite the purchase of silver by the Treasury, the price of that metal continued to fall. At the same time, gold, which was more valuable, was disappearing. It was hoarded by nervous businessmen or sent to Europe. Recall Gresham's law: Cheap money drives the more valuable money out of circulation. Treasury purchases of silver were made by giving the sellers silver certificates. This paper money could be exchanged for gold. When the government issued bonds, they were sold for gold, which the Treasury badly needed. But as soon as the buyer of bonds got them, he could sell them for paper money, which he exchanged for gold. As gold continued to flow out of the Treasury, rumors swept Europe that the United States would be forced to cease gold payments. These rumors caused a further sale of American bonds by foreign bankers and increased the flow of gold to

[45]

After the Panic of 1893 broke, President Cleveland blamed the country's troubles on the Sherman Silver Purchase Act and finally got Congress to repeal it. Louis Dalrymple in Puck *pictures Uncle Sam rescuing "Business Interests" from the "Silver Flood."*

Europe. Businessmen waited anxiously — hoping for the best but fearing the worst. Indeed, business confidence began to go into hiding along with gold.

Within two months after Cleveland took office, the panic was on. The President blamed the nation's troubles on the Sherman Act and called Congress into special session to repeal it. Democratic and Republican newspapers in the East and Midwest praised the President. They said his prompt action would restore "business confidence," which had been shaken by the draining of gold from the Treasury and by free silver's threat to "sound money." The free-silver forces, led by Representatives William Jennings Bryan and "Silver Dollar Dick" Bland, bitterly defended the Sherman Act. The Republicans took little part in the debate. They stood by gleefully and watched the battling Democrats cripple their own party. Then the helpful Republicans joined antisilver Democrats to repeal an act that had, after all, been passed by a Republican-controlled Congress. The furious Bland told Cleveland that Eastern and Western Democrats had come to "a parting of the ways."

Repeal of the Sherman Act did not end the depression. Nor did it end the Treasury's gold problem. Large numbers of silver certificates, which had been issued while the Sherman Act was in force, were still in circulation. Holders of this paper money took it to the Treasury and demanded gold. The continued sale of American bonds by European bankers also drained more gold from the Treasury. Soon, the Treasury's gold reserve fell below 100 million dollars. The worried President feared that in time the government would be unable to pay gold on demand. He believed this would ruin the government's credit and deepen the depression. Secretary of the Treasury John Carlisle began selling government bonds for gold. But the buyers of these bonds paid for them with gold that they got *from* the Treasury. This "endless chain" drained gold from the Treasury faster than it was being replaced by bond sales. Cleveland

[47]

This anti-Cleveland cartoon by Victor in Judge *shows the President trying to make the gold reserve "thermometer" rise. The sale of government bonds for gold, which was aided by J. P. Morgan, increased the reserves but did nothing to end the depression.*

then sought the aid of a group of Wall Street bankers headed by J. P. Morgan and August Belmont. They broke the "endless chain" by arranging to get from Europe most of the gold they used to pay for government bonds. Free-silver Democrats and Populists accused Cleveland of selling out to the Wall Street bankers. But the President insisted that he had acted for the good of the nation.

When Congress assembled for its regular session in December, 1893, Cleveland urged it to revise the McKinley Tariff. The Wilson Tariff, which was passed by the House, reduced the duties on many products. However, this reasonably good bill was ripped to pieces in the Senate by protection-minded Democrats led by Senator Gorman of Maryland. After eight months of wrangling, the House finally accepted a bill now called the Wilson-Gorman Tariff. It contained 634 Senate changes, most of them bad. Cleveland long had contended that "a tariff for any other purpose than public revenue is public robbery." He declared that the failure to pass a strong tariff reform bill "means party perfidy and party dishonor." This criticism brought a savage counterattack by Democratic senators. Believing that the Wilson-Gorman Tariff was at least better than the McKinley Tariff, Cleveland let it become a law without his signature. At the end of this session of Congress, Western Democrats were growling at Eastern Democrats, and both groups were snarling at the President.

The Wilson-Gorman Tariff contained one provision that pleased farmers and workers. This levied a 2 percent tax on all incomes over $4,000 a year. (Such a tax had been proposed by the Populists in 1892.) During the Civil War, Congress had imposed an income tax, which had since been repealed. In 1880, the Supreme Court had ruled this tax constitutional, but the new tax was quickly challenged by a group of rich Easterners. Big business lawyer Joseph Choate called the tax an attack on thrift by the disrupters of society. He warned that if the Court approved it "then the communistic march goes on. . . ." By a five to four vote, the Supreme Court ruled the income tax unconstitutional. Chief Justice Melvin Fuller said that, under the Constitution, all taxes must be uniform; everybody must pay the same amount. The government could not require the rich to pay more than the poor.

Supporting Fuller's opinion, Justice Stephen Field grumpily warned: "The present assault on capital is but the beginning. It will be but the stepping-stone to others, larger and more sweeping, till our political contests will become a war of the poor against the rich; a war constantly growing in intensity and bitterness. . . ."

The great liberal justice, John Marshall Harlan, angrily dissented: "This decision may well excite the gravest apprehension. . . . No tax is more just in its essence than an income tax. . . . On my conscience, I regard this decision as a disaster."

The New York *World* wrote that "the overthrow of the income tax is the triumph of selfishness over patriotism. Great and rich corporations, by . . . fighting against a petty tax . . . have secured the exemption of wealth from paying its just share toward the support of the government that protects it." Few decisions of the Court have been more bitterly criticized. Farmers and workers were convinced that the Court could not be trusted to give a poor man justice. The income tax finally was legalized by the ratification by the states of the Sixteenth Amendment in 1913.

The year following the panic, 1894, was one of the bleakest Americans have ever known. Wages hit rock bottom. Wheat sold for 49 cents a bushel; cotton, for 5 cents a pound. Hungry, jobless men roamed the land, begging food and sometimes stealing. At night, the fires of their hobo camps flickered endlessly across the land. Ragged, shivering men in Chicago insulted policemen or smashed store windows in order to be put in jail where it was warm and where they would be given food. Mark Hanna walked the windswept streets of Cleveland and quietly handed out money to shabby men. To an attorney in New York, Hanna wrote: "The situation here is terrible. We are not in as bad shape as Chicago. H—— tells me that our friend B—— is in a bad way and is likely to go into bankruptcy. Take enclosed [check] to him and tell him to hang on."

Coxey's Army

In Washington, the Senate and House wrangled over the Wilson-Gorman Tariff. Populists accused Democrats and Republicans of taking secret payments to prevent tariff changes that might hurt big business. The newspapers began running stories about "Coxey's army." Jacob S. Coxey, a rich quarry owner of Massillon, Ohio, had proposed that the government issue 500 million dollars in paper money to pay for the building of better roads. He said this program would give jobs to the unemployed and provide an increased supply of money that people could use to pay their debts. Coxey announced that he would lead his "Army of the Commonwealth" to Washington to ask Congress and the President for help. Accompanied by his son, Legal Tender Coxey, and his wife, Coxey started from Massillon with 100 men. They were trailed by 47 newspaper men who regularly reported on the progress of the "General" and his "army." Most newspapers treated the whole affair as a huge joke, but Coxey was no wild-eyed dreamer. His program was similar to that used by President Franklin D. Roosevelt during the depression of the 1930s. In 1894, however, unemployment was looked upon as "an act of God." Most Democratic and Republican leaders believed the government should not get involved in unemployment relief or other measures to aid the people or business.

[52]

Jacob S. Coxey proposed that the government issue paper money to build better roads and provide jobs for the unemployed. When "General Coxey" and his "army" got to Washington, he was arrested for "trespassing on the grass," as shown in this drawing by T. Dart Walker in Harper's Weekly.

President Cleveland was not a cruel man, but he agreed that the government should stand aside and let things work themselves out. Business would improve as time went by. During his first administration, Cleveland had vetoed a $10,000 appropriation for distributing seed grain in Texas counties suffering from a drought. He wrote: ". . . Federal aid in such cases encourages the expectation of paternal care on the part of the

[53]

government and weakens the sturdiness of our national character. The lessons of paternalism ought to be unlearned, and the better lessons taught that while the people should patriotically and cheerfully support their government, its functions do not include the support of the people."

In these days before organized welfare systems in the cities, the suffering of the unemployed and their families was terrible. Fathers sat in ramshackle houses, looking at their fretful, hungry children and cursing helplessly. Private charity alone was expected to do what it could to feed and clothe the needy. As for the hordes of wandering tramps, the Chicago *Tribune* earlier had suggested that it might be a good idea to give them poisoned food.

This attitude of the government toward aid to the jobless and business did not change until the depression of the 1930s. Then, Republican President Herbert Hoover approved aid to hard-pressed business. Later, Democratic President Roosevelt's New Deal launched a broad program of aid to the jobless, business, and agriculture.

On May 1, Coxey's "army," now numbering about 300 men, marched to the Capitol in Washington while thousands of curious citizens watched. When Coxey and two of his associates walked on the lawn, they were arrested "for trespassing on the grass." For this offense, and for displaying a banner without a permit, the three men were jailed for 20 days. By the time Coxey was released, his discouraged followers had scattered.

The Pullman Strike

While Coxey's men were marching in Washington, the Pullman Palace Car Company ordered a 20 percent cut in the wages of workers in its shops. They were located in a Chicago suburb controlled by and named for this maker of railroad sleeping cars. Pullman owned the stores, the power plant, and the workers' houses. Rents were high and the prices in the stores outrageous. It was estimated that after paying his rent a worker had about 75 cents a day to feed and clothe his family. When spokesmen for the workers asked George B. Pullman for lower rents or higher wages, he denied their request and fired the spokesmen. Immediately, 2,500 men quit work and the shops were closed.

Mayors of nearby cities, as well as prominent businessmen, begged Pullman to arbitrate. He flatly declared he had nothing to discuss with his workers. William McKinley sent his brother Abner to talk to Pullman. The industrialist's stubbornness sent Abner storming out of his home in a rage.

Many of Pullman's workers belonged to the A. F. of L.'s American Railway Union, headed by Eugene V. Debs. When the company refused to discuss the strike with the union, the union ordered its members not to handle trains carrying Pullman cars. This sympathy strike tied up all but 6 of the 24 railroads entering Chicago. The General Managers'

[55]

When workers of the Pullman Car Company struck against wage cuts, they were supported by the American Railway Union, and soon all but six of twenty-four railroads entering Chicago were tied up. Insisting that the mail must move, President Cleveland sent troops to Chicago and they clashed with the strikers. (Drawing by C. W. Peters from a sketch by G. A. Coffin, in Harper's Weekly.)

Association of the railroads now went to the aid of Pullman, and the strike became more than simply a dispute between Pullman and his workers. The railroads were determined to challenge the power of the American Railway Union.

In Cleveland, Mark Hanna upset a group of business associates in the Union Club by shouting: "What in God's name does Pullman think he's doing? A man is a damn fool who won't meet his men half way!" One businessman mildly commented that Pullman deserved credit for building a model town for his workers.

"Oh, hell!" snorted Hanna. "Go live in Pullman and find out how much Pullman gets sellin' city water and gas ten percent higher to those poor fools!"

Attorney General Richard Olney, a former railroad lawyer, now stepped into the tense situation in Chicago. He got a Federal judge to issue a "blanket injunction" against union officials, which ordered them to stop obstructing the railroads and delaying the mails. The strikers ignored the injunction. Debs, who was a gentle man, urged his union members to avoid violence, but trains were derailed and railroad shops burned. Charges were made that the General Managers' Association secretly hired thugs to rip up tracks and destroy property to discredit the strikers.

Urged on by Attorney General Olney, President Cleveland ordered Federal troops to Chicago to see that the mail trains moved. Governor Altgeld of Illinois protested that "Federal troops can do nothing that the state troops cannot do." Cleveland lost his temper and said that "if it takes the entire army and navy of the United States to deliver a post card in Chicago that card will be delivered." A regiment of U.S. regulars entered Chicago and immediately clashed with strikers. Seven men were killed and dozens wounded. Governor Altgeld charged that the army had stirred up disorder instead of ending it, but he got no support from the newspapers and the public. Altgeld's defense of labor's rights and his attack on the courts when he pardoned the anarchists accused of the Haymarket bombing already had turned conservatives against him.

While Federal troops patrolled Chicago, agents of the railroads went into crowds of jobless men, offering five dollars a day for workers in the yards and stations. There were plenty of unemployed men in Chicago at this time. The World's Fair of 1893 had lured thousands of men to the city, and in 1894 many of them were hunting for work.

On July 17, Debs and three other strike leaders were arrested for obstructing the mails, and the strike quickly collapsed. The men were forced to return to work on terms offered by the railroads. The Pullman company won, although a committee appointed by President Cleveland criticized company officials and cleared the union of any wrongdoing. But on December 14, the Federal circuit court found Debs and his associates guilty of contempt for defying an injunction. Debs was sent to prison for six months; his two associates for three. In its decision, the court said the Sherman Anti-Trust Act could be used against unions if they were engaged in "a conspiracy to hinder and obstruct interstate commerce." Debs appealed his case to the Supreme Court, but it ruled against him.

The arrest of Debs and the Cleveland-Altgeld quarrel convinced labor that the President had sent troops to Chicago to break a strike, not to preserve order and move the mail. The use, for the first time, of a "blanket injunction" against a union also aroused widespread criticism in the newspapers.

The Debs case and the income tax case were two of three cases that proved to workers and farmers that the Supreme Court was firmly on the side of the rich and powerful. The third case involved the government's attempt to enforce the Sherman Anti-Trust Act against the sugar trust, as "a conspiracy in restraint of trade." The Supreme Court ruled that

[58]

this trust, which controlled 98 percent of the sugar refining in the nation, was a "local" business. It was not directly involved in interstate commerce and therefore could not be controlled by the federal government. Farmers and workers bitterly protested this decision, but Attorney General Olney shrugged off all complaints. "I see the Government lost," he wrote. "I assumed it would, and that is why I have not prosecuted under a law I believe is no good." The Sherman Act was "no good" when aimed at business, but it was "good" when used to attack a labor union.

The party in power during a depression is sure to be blamed for all the ills of the nation. In addition, Cleveland's deal with Morgan to buy gold and his sending of troops to Chicago during the Pullman strike hurt the Democratic party during the 1894 election. The Democrats suffered a crushing defeat and their membership in the House was cut to 104, as against 248 Republicans. The number of Democrats in the Senate was cut from 42 to 39. The Populist vote increased 42 percent and they elected seven representatives and six senators. The jubilant Republicans boasted that in the 1896 presidential election they could "nominate a rag-baby or a yellow dog and elect it."

The year of 1895 was another one of grinding misery for the jobless and the hard-pressed farmers. It also was a time of short tempers. A boundary dispute between British Guiana and Venezuela had flared in 1887, and Britain had rejected all efforts by the United States to settle it. Finally, in 1895, Richard Olney, now Secretary of State, told the British that their presence in South America was "unnatural." When the British Foreign Minister hinted rather strongly that his nation's quarrel with Venezuela was none of America's business, President Cleveland reacted violently. He got Congress to vote money for a commission to settle the boundary dispute. Then he advised Britain that efforts to take territory from Venezuela would be looked upon by the United States "as a willful aggression against its rights. . . ." The New York *Sun* ran a headline pro-

[59]

In 1895, Britain declared that its boundary dispute with Venezuela was none of the United States business. President Cleveland sent a sharp message to Congress, and war fever rose in the country. Homer C. Davenport has Uncle Sam "Getting the Old Gun Ready." Cooler heads in Britain and the United States worked out an agreement that settled the quarrel.

claiming WAR IF NECESSARY. Theodore Roosevelt wrote to Senator Henry Cabot Lodge: "The bankers, brokers and anglomaniacs generally . . ." seemed to want "peace at any price. . . . Personally, I rather hope the fight will come soon. The clamor of the peace faction has convinced me that this country needs a war."

The grinding depression appears to have made many people willing to look upon war as a relief from their troubles. One senator even said that "war would be a good thing even if we get whipped!" Cooler heads in both Britain and the United States reasoned that a war between the two English-speaking nations would be a crime. Britain signed a treaty with Venezuela, and an arbitration committee was appointed to fix the boundary.

During 1895, the Republicans controlled Congress but lacked enough votes to pass any important legislation. Western Republicans, who favored silver, refused to support a tariff bill because Eastern Republicans would not back a free-silver bill. Actually, Republican leaders were not unhappy about this deadlock. It enabled the party to delay taking a stand on the hot issues stirring the nation until the Republican convention in 1896.

Meanwhile, the Democrats were having nothing but trouble. Cleveland had to sell more bonds to protect the Treasury's gold reserve. This move, which gave Wall Street bankers a neat profit, infuriated Western Democrats. Eastern Democrats from industrial states still fumed over Cleveland's stand on the tariff. Labor was bitter over the Pullman strike and the imprisonment of Debs. The President, an honest but stubborn man, did not have the knack of finding a common ground where men of differing views could meet and work together. He lacked the patience to lead jealous, suspicious men; he issued orders and demanded that they be followed. Now Bryan, Bland, and other free-silver leaders challenged Cleveland's control of the party. Cleveland insisted that Bryan really

[61]

was not a Democrat. "Bryan's mind, training and imagination," said Cleveland, "all combine to make him a Populist. . . ." Bryan and his followers replied that Cleveland had turned into a Republican. Cleveland insisted that he had not changed but that the Democratic party had changed by welcoming the Populists and their ideas.

William Jennings Bryan, as he appeared in the mid-1890s.

The Making of a President

In 1892, when the Democrats were riding high, few Republicans wanted their party's nomination for the Presidency. They figured, correctly, that Cleveland could not be beaten. But as Democratic prospects sank in 1895, the Republican nomination for 1896 became a prize worth seeking. Several Republican leaders, Senator William Allison of Iowa, Senator Shelby Cullom of Illinois, former Vice-President Levi P. Morton of New York, and Speaker of the House Thomas P. Reed of Maine, began to seek support. They found that Governor William McKinley of Ohio was already far ahead of them in the race for the big prize.

After his defeat in 1890, McKinley had returned home and was elected governor in 1891. On the advice of Mark Hanna, he shunned the Republican nomination for President in 1892. The next year, he was re-elected governor by over 80,000 votes. McKinley was a fairly good governor and won a reputation as a prolabor man. During the 1894 election campaign, McKinley made 371 speeches in sixteen states. He spoke for the party, but he also let the voters get acquainted with McKinley. Opposition to the McKinley Tariff had softened in four years, and he found that the slogan, "Bill McKinley of the McKinley Bill," had some pulling power.

In January, 1895, Mark Hanna, who had made a fortune in coal, iron, and Great Lakes shipping, retired from business and went into a new line of work. He planned to make William McKinley President of the United States. Hanna had first noticed McKinley in 1876. During a strike in one of Hanna's mines, strikebreakers were hired and violence flared. The state militia was called out and one striker was killed in a riot. When twenty-five rioting miners were brought to trial, they were defended by young William McKinley. Though McKinley had to buck adverse public opinion against the miners, only one man was convicted. Years later, Hanna said that McKinley's actions during the trial convinced him of the young lawyer's courage and ability. The clash at Hanna's mine also taught him the need for arbitration in labor disputes. He never had another strike in any of his businesses. An official of the Miners' National Association stated that Hanna "was the first mining operator . . . to recognize the cardinal principle of arbitration in the settlement of wage disputes. . . ."

It was Hanna's attitude toward labor that caused him to explode angrily against George Pullman. He wanted business and labor to work together, and he feared that stubborn men like Pullman would make such teamwork impossible. Although Hanna's labor policies were liberal for his time, he still was a tough businessman who believed that what was good for business was good for the country. If business prospered, then labor would gain too. As a political boss, Hanna followed the same line: he got generous contributions from businessmen by promising them that Republicans in government would follow policies favorable to business.

McKinley agreed with Hanna that business and labor must work together. But he was less outspoken than the Cleveland millionaire. Foes said that McKinley's kindly manner concealed a softness and a lack of strong feeling. Theodore Roosevelt once exploded that McKinley had "the backbone of a chocolate eclair." But McKinley appears to have had the toughness and good sense not to let dishonest men use him.

[64]

For his times, Mark Hanna was a farsighted businessman, and he was deeply hurt by cartoons that showed him as a cruel, greedy capitalist. (George B. Luks in The Verdict.*)*

In 1895, Hanna rented a winter home in Georgia where he entertained Southern politicians and lined up support for McKinley in the coming Republican convention. Later that year, Hanna went east to meet the New York Republican boss, Tom Platt, and the Pennsylvania boss, Matt Quay. He then told McKinley that the bosses would support him if McKinley agreed, in writing, to appoint Platt Secretary of the Treasury. McKinley balked and Hanna merely smiled and said, "We have got to work harder." Hanna worked so hard lining up convention votes that McKinley's chief opponent, Speaker of the House Tom Reed, was reduced to making nasty remarks. Asked about his chances for the nomination, the razor-tongued Reed snapped: "The convention could do worse, and probably will." Commenting on McKinley's early support of free silver, and his silence on the subject before the convention, Reed said: "McKinley does not want to be called a goldbug or a silverbug, so he has compromised on a straddlebug."

McKinley easily won the nomination on the first ballot. Garret Hobart of New Jersey was then nominated for the vice-presidency. The big fight in the convention at St. Louis was over "sound money." Hanna had prowled among the delegates and found a majority favoring the gold standard. He reported this by phone to McKinley in Canton, Ohio. McKinley wanted to dodge the money question and center his campaign on the tariff. But Hanna convinced him that it would be wise to back the gold-standard men. The party platform plank on money was a shrewdly worded statement that held out hope for bimetallism (the use of both gold and silver) through an international agreement, but flatly declared that until then, "the existing gold standard must be preserved." When this statement was read, Senator Henry M. Teller of Colorado, the leader of the silver forces, leaped to his feet to demand the substitution of a free-silver pledge. The gray-haired Teller, a founder of the party, begged delegates not to desert the cause of silver and then sat down weeping.

[66]

Cannon of Utah then took the floor and threatened to walk out of the convention. Fearing that Teller and Cannon might swing many delegates to their cause, Hanna bellowed, "Go! Go!" When Cannon repeated his threat, Hanna screamed, "Good-bye!" Other gold-standard men took up this chant and Teller led thirty-five silver men out of the hall. Aside from the gold plank, the platform promised to strengthen the tariff, grant liberal pensions to veterans, and establish a national board to arbitrate labor disputes.

The free-silver men, led by Bryan and Bland, lost no time in taking control of the Democratic convention in Chicago. Rejecting a resolution praising the work of the Cleveland administration, the party platform opposed practically every policy of the President. It demanded "the free and unlimited coinage of both silver and gold at the present legal ratio of sixteen to one, without waiting for the aid or consent of any other nation." The platform condemned Cleveland's bond-selling policy, the use of injunctions in labor disputes, and the sending of troops to Chicago during the Pullman strike — another slap at Cleveland. Other platform planks called for stricter regulation of the railroads, a constitutional amendment authorizing an income tax, pensions for veterans, and a tariff for revenue only.

A minority report on the platform condemned the adoption of bi-metallism by the United States alone and praised the Cleveland administration. This touched off a bitter debate on the convention floor. Trembling with rage, Senator David B. Hill of New York, a foe of free silver, protested against "unusual, unwise and revolutionary steps" that would drive many men out of the party. Senator "Pitchfork Ben" Tillman defended free silver and called Cleveland "a tool of Wall Street."

The 20,000 sweltering men and women in the convention hall were getting a bit anxious and restless when William Jennings Bryan rose to make the final speech on the party platform. Bryan had served two terms

[67]

in the House and had been defeated for election to the Senate in 1894. Then he had gone to work, rallying support for free silver and quietly winning votes for his party's presidential nomination.

Bryan's opening words, delivered in that marvelous mellow voice of his, caught and held the attention of his audience. "It would be presumptuous, indeed, to present myself against the distinguished gentlemen to whom you have listened if this were a mere measure of abilities; but this is not a contest between persons. The humblest citizen in all the land, when clad in the armor of a righteous cause, is stronger than all the hosts of error. I come to speak to you in defense of a cause as holy as the cause of liberty — the cause of humanity."

Naming those for whom he spoke — the wage earner, the country lawyer, the small merchant, the farmer, the miner — Bryan declared: "We come not as aggressors. Ours is not a war of conquest. We are fighting in defense of our homes, our families and our posterity. We have petitioned and our petitions have been scorned. We have entreated and our entreaties have been disregarded. We have begged and they have mocked us when our calamity came. We beg no longer; we entreat no more; we petition no more. We defy them. . . ."

The final words of Bryan's speech — one of the most memorable in American history — brought the crowd roaring to its feet.

". . . Having behind us the producing masses of the nation and the world, supported by the commercial interests, the labor interests and the toilers everywhere, we will answer their demand for a gold standard by saying to them: 'You shall not press down upon the brow of labor this crown of thorns, you shall not crucify mankind upon a cross of gold.'"

Bryan's speech put him in the lead for the presidential nomination, but it took five ballots before he defeated "Silver Dollar Dick" Bland. The convention then made a peace offering to the East by nominating for the vice-presidency Arthur M. Sewall of Maine. Sewall was president of a

[68]

bank and a shipbuilding firm and favored the protective tariff, but he had recently become a supporter of free silver.

Conservative Democrats looked upon the nomination of Bryan as a disaster. "Are you still a Democrat?" a friend asked Senator Hill when he returned from the convention. "Yes, I am a Democrat still — *very still*," replied Hill. In September, gold Democrats nominated General John M. Palmer as the presidential candidate of the "National Democratic Party." Hanna chortled and said: "The general will get about a hundred thousand votes from Mr. Bryan."

The Populists did not hold their convention until after the Republicans and Democrats had met. They hoped that the goldbugs would gain control of both major parties. Then the free-silver forces, the land reformers, and the friends of labor would swarm to the People's party and carry it to victory in 1896. But Bryan and his silverites upset the plans of the Populists by taking control of the Democratic party and also adopting several planks from the Populist platform of 1892. When the Populists met in St. Louis on July 22, most of their leaders felt there was nothing to do but support Bryan and make free silver the main campaign issue. The delegates nominated Bryan, but one group of Southern rebels refused to accept Sewall. They were given a bit of comfort when Tom Watson of Georgia was nominated for the vice-presidency.

The Populist platform was similar to that of 1892. It also advocated the employment of idle labor on public works in times of depression, and opposed "government by injunction" in labor disputes. But several thoughtful Populist leaders feared that acceptance of free silver as the key issue would shove other more important reforms aside and wreck the party. One foe of Bryan and free silver, Henry Demarest Lloyd, wrote: "The People's party convention in St. Louis was the most discouraging experience in my life. It was not so much that the leaders tricked and bulldozed and betrayed, but that the people submitted. The craze for

[69]

success 'this time' had full possession of them. . . . The free silver movement is a fake. Free silver is the cowbird of the reform movement. It waited until the nest had been built by the sacrifices and labors of others, and then it laid its eggs in it, pushing out the others which lie smashed on the ground."

Republicans were convinced that the fate of the nation depended on the outcome of the election. Republican Senator O. H. Platt thought that Bryan, Altgeld, and Tillman resembled the bloodthirsty leaders of the French Revolution. Theodore Roosevelt told his sister that "this is no mere fight over financial standards. It is a semi-socialistic agrarian movement, with free silver as a mere incident, supported mainly because it is hoped thereby to damage the well to do and thrifty. 'Organized labor' is the chief support of Bryan in the big cities; and his utterances are as criminal as they are wildly silly. All the ugly forces that seethe beneath the social crust are behind him." Roosevelt, who had not forgiven Altgeld for pardoning the anarchists and protesting Cleveland's sending troops to Chicago, refused to meet Altgeld personally. He said he might have to face Altgeld "sword to sword upon the field of battle."

John Hay wrote to Henry Adams in London that "the Boy Orator makes only one speech — but he makes it twice a day. There is no fun in it. He simply reiterates the unquestionable truths that every man who has a clean shirt is a thief and should be hanged, and there is no goodness or wisdom except among the illiterates and criminal classes. . . ."

Mark Hanna went all out to win, but he privately told nervous members of the Union Club: "There won't be a revolution. You are damned fools!"

The Democrats saw the election as a fight between men without money and those with it; between the embattled farmer and the trusts; between the agricultural West and South and the industrial East and Midwest; between silver and gold. Answering charges that he wanted a

[70]

dishonest dollar, Bryan replied: "A dollar approaches honesty as its purchasing power approaches stability." One Democratic campaign song ran:

"You may say what you will of the fifty cent dollar,
But I tell you it beats none at all, all holler."

McKinley and Hanna, who had become chairman of the Republican National Committee, believed the Republican campaign could be waged on the tariff issue alone. Soon, however, alarming reports reached them that Republicans were deserting the party over the silver issue. Hanna finally was convinced that the gold standard had to be defended against the forces of free silver. The word went out to the two headquarters of the party in New York and Chicago. Soon, money was pouring in from every businessman who feared that free silver would ruin him. One railroad gave $50,000. Standard Oil contributed $250,000, and the big Chicago meat packers gave $400,000. The Republican national committee admitted that it had collected $3,500,000, but the total expenditures of the party probably hit $16 million. The silver mining companies contributed to the Democratic party, but it did not have one-tenth of the money muscle that the Republicans had.

Some 25 million copies of 275 different pamphlets, mostly on silver, were distributed by the Republicans. The nation also was plastered with banners, buttons, ribbons, and pictures of McKinley. Hanna made greater use of printing than any campaign manager up to that time. Hanna also sent out 1,400 speakers to talk to labor groups. They were told that the Democrats had caused the depression and that any threat to the gold standard was a threat to workers' jobs.

While Hanna directed a highly efficient organization throughout the country, McKinley stood on his front porch in Canton, Ohio. There, he delivered short speeches, carefully written to contain nothing that would upset the visiting delegations of voters.

[71]

During the 1896 campaign, cartoonist Homer C. Davenport in the New York Journal *pictures William McKinley ("A Man of Mark") under the control of Mark Hanna — complete with dollar signs and antilabor cuff links.*

Traveling night and day, Bryan covered 18,000 miles and delivered hundreds of speeches to vast crowds. Answering charges that the Democrats were to blame for the depression, Bryan said it was caused by the gold standard. He said business would not revive until the nation adopted free silver. Bryan's vigorous campaign began to worry the Republicans, and the attacks on the Democratic candidate became more savage. Denouncing the "Boy Orator of the Platte" as being all mouth and no brains, Republicans compared him to the Platte River: "Five inches deep and five miles wide at the mouth." The New York *Tribune* called him a "wretched, rattle-pated boy, posing in vapid vanity and mouthing resounding rottenness." One minister told his congregation that nobody could be a Christian and vote for the Democratic "anarchists."

The Democrats struck back by calling McKinley a tool of Hanna's, and then concentrated their fire on the Cleveland millionaire. Cartoonist Homer Davenport of the New York *Journal* pictured "Dollar Mark" Hanna as a greedy capitalist with dollar signs on his vest. Tears ran down Hanna's face as he looked at another Davenport cartoon and said: "That hurts . . . to be held up to the gaze of the world as a murderer of women and children. I tell you it hurts."

In September, the Republicans were aided by bumper crops in the West and crop failures in India, which caused farm prices, particularly wheat, to rise. Since Bryan had insisted that prices would not rise under the gold standard, this price upturn cost him the votes of many farmers in the Midwest. Bryan continued, however, to stress free silver, and Hanna contentedly said: "He's talking silver all the time, and that's where we've got him." Bryan had won the support of the A. F. of L., but Samuel Gompers and other labor leaders felt that "the cause of our ills lies far deeper than the question of gold and silver." A law protecting labor's rights against union-busting employers would have been more valuable than silver legislation.

In their appeals to labor, the Republicans promised "a full dinner pail" if McKinley was elected. This promise also was accompanied by a threat. Hundreds of thousands of workers got a slip in their pay envelope the Saturday before election day that said: "If Bryan is elected do not come back to work. The plant will be closed." Senator Teller, who had left the Republican party to support Bryan, shook his head sadly when he

[73]

heard this news. "Boys," he said, "I am afraid that this beats us. If I were a workingman and had nothing but my job, I am afraid that when it came time to vote I would think of the wife and the babies." Democratic charges that Republicans were trying to force labor to vote for McKinley were called "absurd" by Hanna. But this pressure by employers on their workers was so well-organized and widespread that Hanna and other Republican leaders surely knew about it in advance.

McKinley's victory was no landslide, but it was the biggest since Grant beat Horace Greeley in 1872. McKinley got 7,035,638 votes to Bryan's 6,467,946, and 271 electoral votes to Bryan's 176.

The election results showed clearly that the 1896 campaign had pitted the South and West against the East and Midwest, the farmer against the rising industrialist. McKinley easily won the East while Bryan carried the South. McKinley did fairly well in the West, but his victory margin was built up in Ohio, Indiana, Illinois, Wisconsin, and Michigan. Bryan lost because his labor support was too weak to win him any of the heavily populated states in the East and Midwest.

Since Cleveland's victory in 1892 had been almost as sweeping as McKinley's, the Democrats believed they, too, could make a comeback in 1900. They ignored the fact that they had taken a bad beating in 1894 and had not regained any lost ground in 1896. Furthermore, the Republicans were greatly strengthened by the nation's rapid recovery from the depression in 1897 and 1898. Their party became known as the Grand Old Party, and the nickname G.O.P. served as a symbol of good times and prosperity. Until the depression year of 1932, the Republican party could count on a reliable backlog of several million voters who believed it to be the party of prosperity. At the same time, the Democratic party was dubbed the party of depression.

Even before the end of 1896, there were hints of returning prosperity. Encouraged by McKinley's victory, businessmen began to increase

In 1900, the gold standard was adopted by the passage of the Currency Act, and further campaigns for free silver ended. Since farm prices had gone up sharply and prosperity was returning, the farmers made few complaints.

production and hire more workers. The rise of farm prices due to the failure of the Indian wheat crop in 1896 and the shortness of the European wheat crop in 1897 caused farmers to stop worrying about free silver. As in 1879, when a European crop failure helped end the depression of 1873-1879, another disaster abroad hastened U.S. recovery from the depression of 1893-1897. (There is a lesson here for those who feel the U.S. should not concern itself with events elsewhere in the world.)

A sharp increase in the world supply of gold also brought a rise in prices that aided farmers and businessmen. This increase was caused by the discovery of new mines in the Klondike in Alaska and on the Rand in South Africa, and the invention of a new way to obtain gold from low-grade ores. The development of new machines and methods that increased factory production and increased U.S. sales to foreign nations brought more gold into the country and built up the Treasury's reserves of that metal. The amount of money in circulation was increased by government borrowing to pay for the war against Spain in 1898. Increases in the number of immigrants entering the country gave the farmers a bigger market for their crops. When the Currency Act of March 14, 1900, ended further campaigns for free silver by putting the nation firmly on the gold standard, there were few complaints from farmers.

In view of what has happened in the world since the 1930s, the frantic defense of the gold standard in 1896 now looks rather silly to historians. Britain and the United States left the gold standard in 1933 — and the world did not come to an end. One outraged businessman proved to be a bad prophet by moaning: "Well, this is the end of Western civilization."

Historians generally agree that it was unfortunate that the Democrats and Populists risked their fate in 1896 on free silver. The prominence given the money question took attention away from more serious ills that were plaguing the nation. The defeat of Bryan delayed many needed reforms involving the tariff, railroad regulation, labor, control of the trusts, and protection of government lands in the West from lumbering and mining interests. Big business had helped beat Bryan, so big business became a partner of the big Republican party in running the government.

Although the Populists committed suicide by backing Bryan, their reform proposals influenced American politics for many years. The history of the Populists and their ideas shows that the job of third parties is to bring forward proposals that the major parties first denounce and then adopt — later. Republican Presidents Theodore Roosevelt and William H. Taft, and Democrats Woodrow Wilson and Roosevelt, all borrowed ideas from the Populists and got Congress to write them into laws. In the states, governors such as Robert M. LaFollette of Wisconsin were influenced by the Populists. They fought to break the alliance between political bosses and big business and to give the people better government.

Index

[83]

federal troop intervention in, 22, 42, 57

Great Railroad (1877), 21-22

Homestead Steel (1892), 41-43

Pullman (1894), 55-58, 61

Sugar trust, 19, 58-59

"Survival of the fittest" philosophy, 26-27, 29, 43

Sweatshops, 27

Taft, William H., 77

Tariff
early history, 19
of 1864, 19
McKinley (1890), 12, 31, 33, 39, 44, 49, 63
protective, 19, 28, 30-31, 33, 49, 67
Wilson-Gorman (1893), 49, 52

Taxation
income, 35, 49-50
surplus, 30

Teller, Henry M., 66-67, 73-74

Tillman, "Pitchfork Ben," 34, 41, 67, 70

Timber Culture Act of 1873, 36

Timber and Stone Act of 1878, 36-37

Trusts, 17-19, 58-59
defined, 17

Unemployment of 1894, 4, 50, 52, 54

Union Pacific Railroad, 4

Unions, 20-25, 28

American Federation of Labor, 21, 24-25, 41, 55

collective bargaining, 20, 21, 24

early history, 20-22

industrial *vs.* craft, 22, 24

Knights of Labor, 21-24

use of Anti-Trust Act against, 58

See also Strikes

U.S. Supreme Court
Debs case ruling of, 58
and ICC decisions, 15
income tax rulings of, 49-50, 58
Munn v. Illinois, 15
and Sherman Anti-Trust Act, 58-59
Wabash Railroad v. Illinois, 15

Venezuelan controversy with Britain, 59, 61

Veterans' pensions, 30, 44, 67

Wabash Railroad v. Illinois, 15

Wabash railway system, 23

Wages, 20, 22, 41, 44, 50
disputes 23, 24
scrip, 27-28

Watson, Tom, 41, 69

Weaver, James B., 38, 40

Wheat prices, 5, 31, 50

Wilson-Gorman Tariff of 1893, 49, 52

Wilson, Woodrow, 77

Workers. *See* Labor